Harley, the Therapy Dog: How He Became a Hero

Joan Murray

ISBN 979-8-89043-138-7 (paperback)
ISBN 979-8-89130-165-8 (hardcover)
ISBN 979-8-89043-139-4 (digital)

Christian Faith Publishing
832 Park Avenue
Meadville, PA 16335
www.christianfaithpublishing.com

Printed in the United States of America

For my mother (RIP), who wanted me to write this book.

For Mr. Mike (and family), a great dog trainer.
For the St. James Veterinary Medical Center (great medical care)
For Susan Hinkle (MO Patriot Paws) and
Susan Aspeotes (Red Cross Therapy Dogs)—
great friends and mentors
For Billy Jean Walker—her volunteer work introduced
me to Harley (scheduled to be put down the next
day) and Sophia (my next therapy dog)

God is good.

Ms. Joan loved Harley very much. She adopted him from a local shelter after she retired from the military. But Harley got sick. He had cancer, and to save him, the doctors amputated (cut off) part of his paw.

After his surgery, Harley had trouble going to the vet. He was afraid. Harley was also very sad because he wanted to be a good dog. A friend suggested dog training. So they went to see Mr. Mike, the dog trainer.

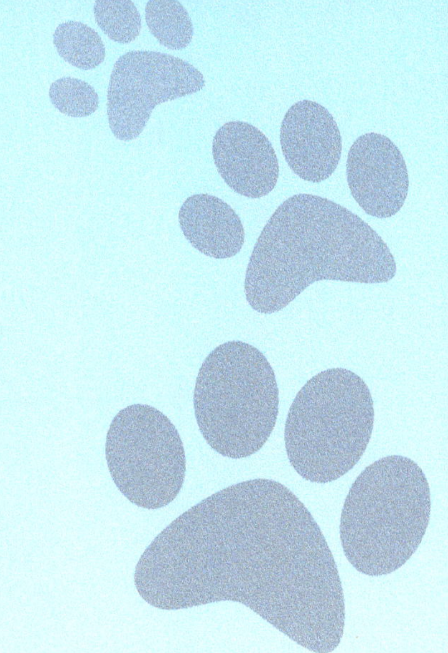

Ms. Joan was afraid too. So she prayed before class, practice, and visits. Ms. Joan knew how important it was for Harley to get over his fears.

Mr. Mike taught Harley how to be a good dog. "Sit." "Stay." He gained Harley's trust. Mr. Mike also taught Ms. Joan how to be a good owner. "Loose leash." "Have him walk close to you." And within three weeks, Harley was unafraid. Mr. Mike mentioned the therapy dog program, and Ms. Joan knew what they wanted to become.

Harley passed his tests and became a therapy dog. He knew that he was a good dog and that Ms. Joan was proud of him.

Harley and Ms. Joan became a therapy dog team.

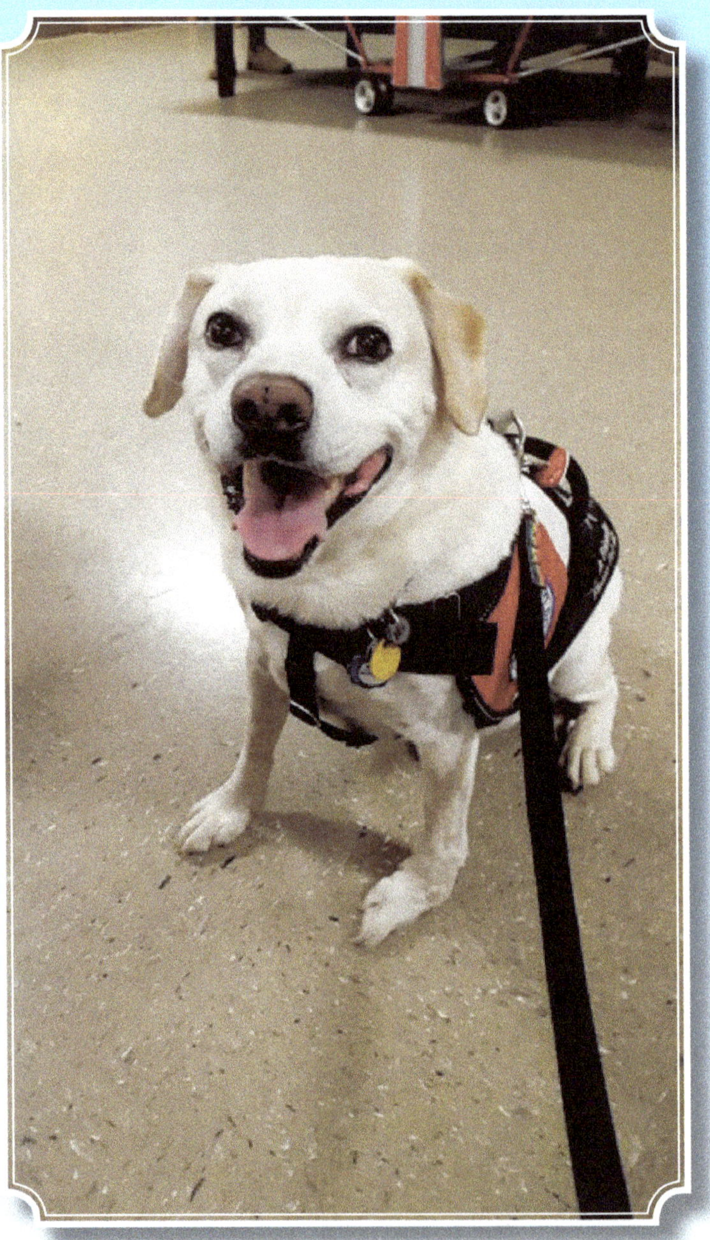

Harley was happy. He learned that even with half a paw, he was valuable.

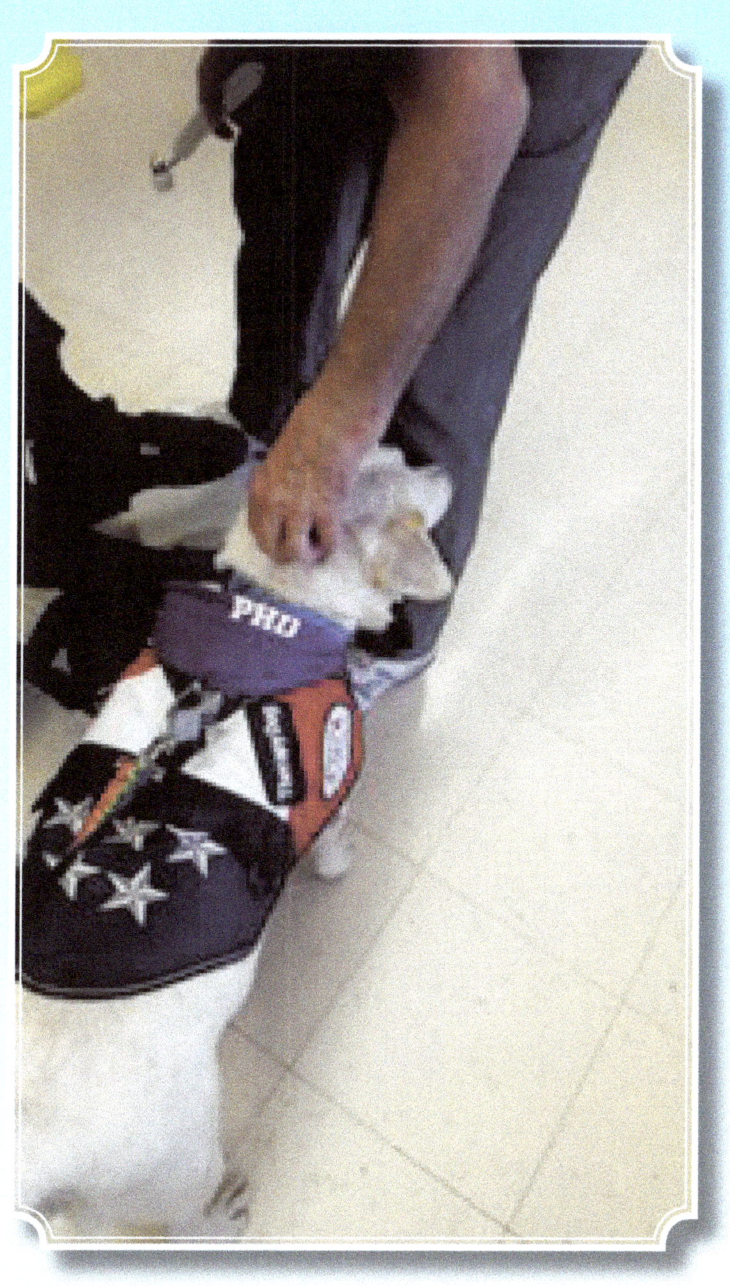

Harley and Ms. Joan visited the veterans' home. Harley was very helpful.

Harley made new friends.

Harley went to VBS (Vacation Bible School).

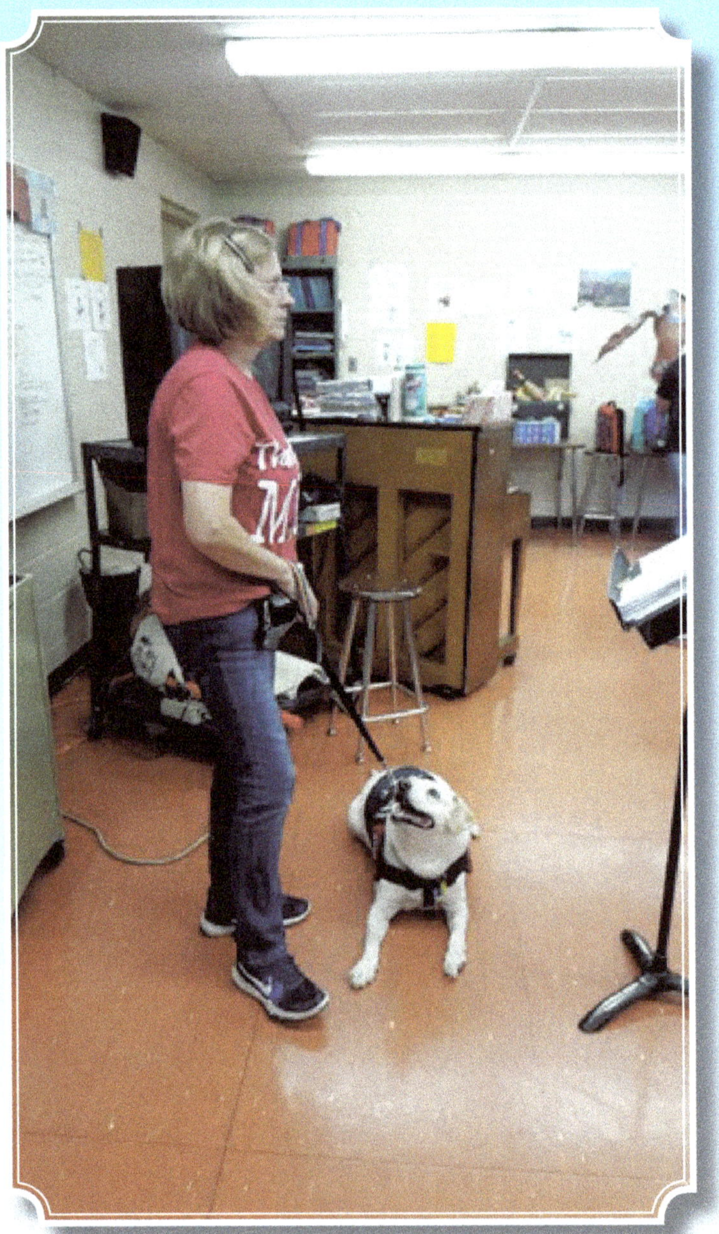

Harley helped Ms. Joan at school. He even liked the drums!

Harley had fun visiting all their friends.

Ms. Joan's friends made shirts for her!

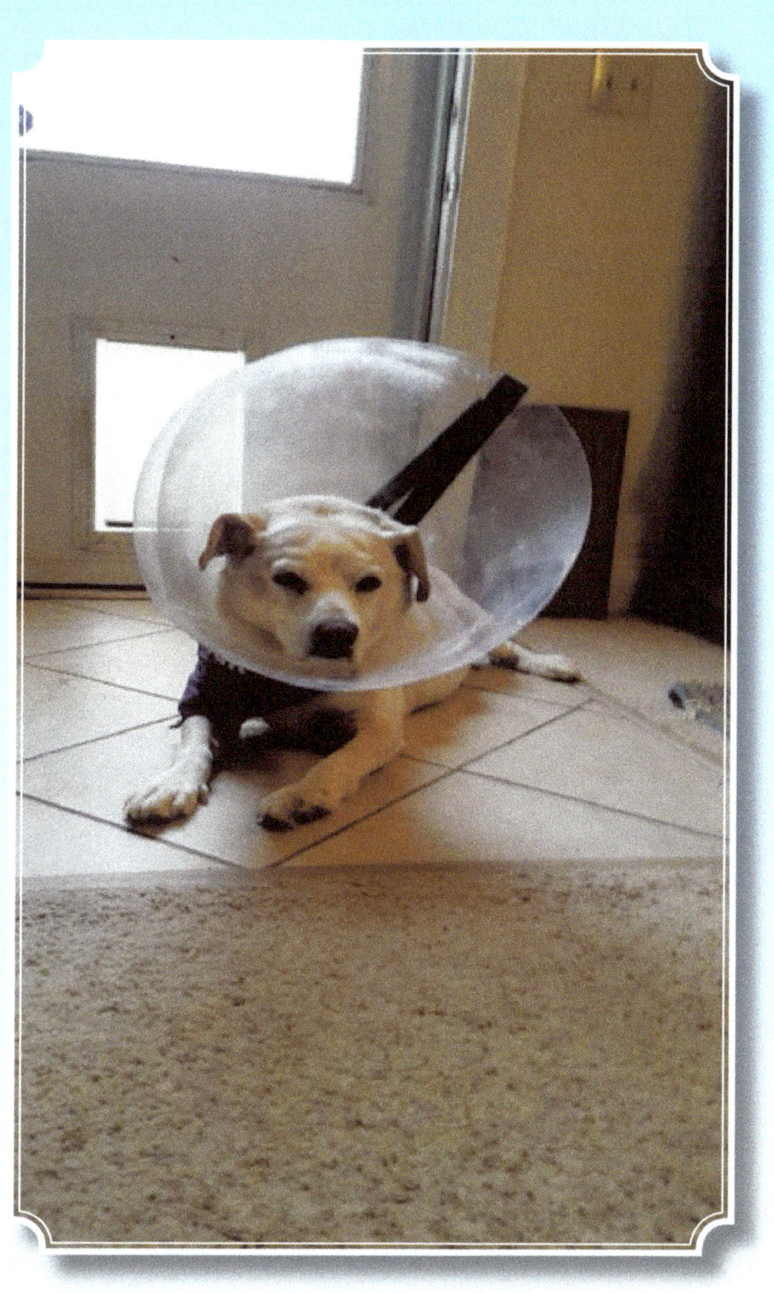

But Harley was still getting sick.

Harley earned his Therapy Dog Excellent Title (200 visits) and was nominated for the Hero Dog Award. He was on TV!

https://www.ky3.com/content/news/Leighs-Lost-and-Found-Vote-now-for-a-local-rescue-mutt-to-win-a-national-therapy-dog-award-477562893.html

Harley was in a magazine.
But he was having trouble breathing.

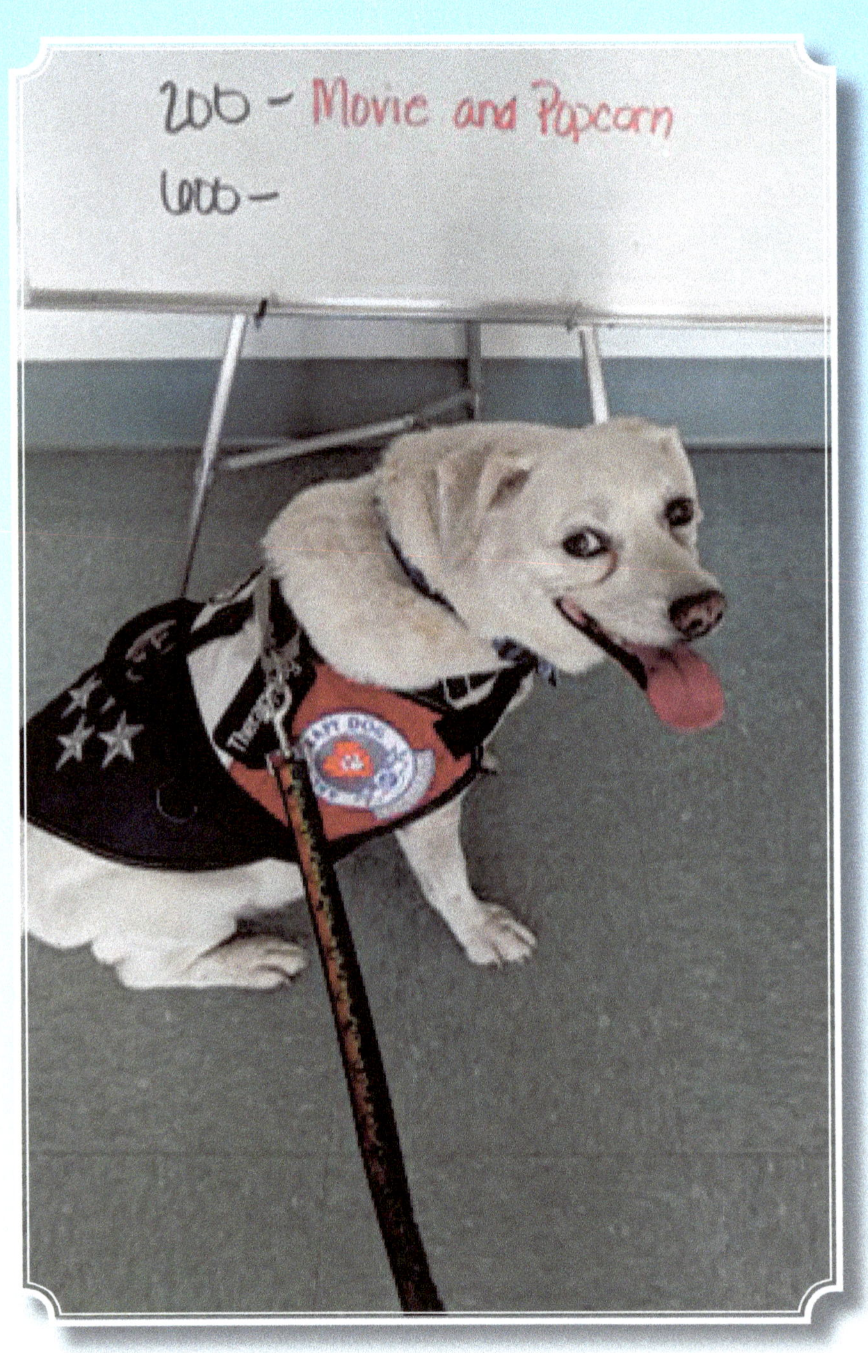

Harley's last visit.

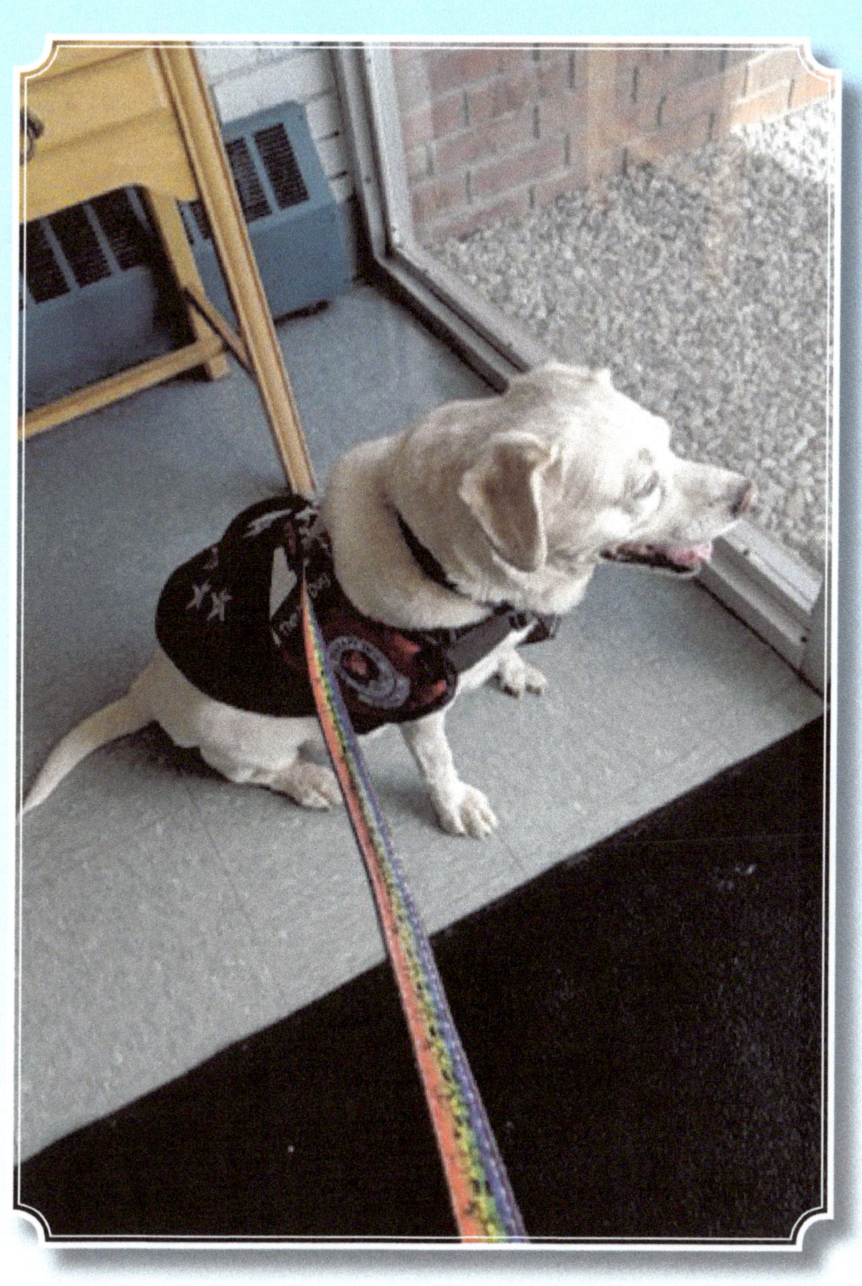

Harley's cancer was back.

He passed away on September 21, 2018.

People were kind to Ms. Joan. But she was sad. Ms. Joan had lost her best friend.

Ms. Joan really missed Harley, but she wanted to give a dog a home that needed one. And another story began.

About the Author

Joan Murray was raised in Somerville, New Jersey, and was the middle of five children. Dr. Murray's mother was a nurse and the most influential person in her life. She encouraged Joan to complete her doctorate and wanted her to write the children's book about Harley, something Dr. Murray did after her mother's death in November 2022.

Although Dr. Murray was raised in New Jersey, she settled in Richland, Missouri, after retirement from the military. Her closest companions are her rescue therapy dogs. Dr. Murray and her current therapy dog, Sophia, have currently completed 346 visits and are working on Sophia's Therapy Dog Distinguished Title. As a therapy dog team, Sophia and Joan volunteer at Phelps County Hospital, Parkside Assisted Living Facility, and Rolla Middle School, where Dr. Murray teaches music.

Joan Murray attended Northwestern University on a music scholarship. Dr. Murray entered the military in 1985 and retired in 2005 after serving as the 399th Army Band (Fort Leonard Wood) Enlisted Bandleader. Ms. Murray adopted Harley the summer of 2005 after retiring from the military. Harley was her faithful companion as Dr. Murray became a certified music teacher, through the Troops to Teachers Program. Through the military, Dr. Murray learned the importance of good leadership and decided to complete her doctoral work on the Teacher Leader program (leading students through classroom teaching). Ms. Murray taught in two previous districts before her current assignment at Rolla Middle School. Harley passed away in September of her first year there.